GIRL
READ
YOUR
BIBLE

Encouraging the Search for Biblical Truth

BY HONEY WOODS

CONTENTS

INTRODUCTION

It seems as though generations of believers, those who proudly call themselves Christians, are growing up without truly knowing what it means to follow Jesus. We say that we follow Him, but do we actually know what that looks like? Perhaps some of us have chosen to base our Christianity off a weekly Bible lesson, a sermon we heard, or maybe a song on Christian radio. But where should we be looking to know what it means to follow Jesus, to live a life that emulates His? What are we doing calling ourselves Christians, not knowing Who Christ is or what He did?

I grew up in church, in attendance practically every Sunday since I was born. I went to a private Christian school, learning the Bible inside and out and even attended a Christian University. I volunteered in virtually every church I've gone to in some way, shape, or form. I had a reputation of being the "good kid," the one no one doubted was a Christian. I memorized the Bible verses, sang the songs about Jesus, bought the Christian CDs, and always tried to do the "right" thing. But what I didn't truly comprehend for many of those years was that virtually none of that meant anything.

Looking back now, I think perhaps I was often simply going through the motions of what I thought it meant to be a Christian; and I would guess that I'm not the only one who can relate to that. I had a list of things, even good, well-intentioned, "Christian things" that I continued to check off an imaginary list of what being a Christian was. I'm a self-proclaimed perfectionist by nature so I wanted to be the best, to feel like I was doing everything "just right" to make God proud, to earn His acceptance. But the reality is that is not what He desired from me at all. His love wasn't something I had to earn. How do I know that? How do any of us find out what God's desire is for our lives as Christ followers? We need to be in the Word.

We have been blessed with wonderful, eloquent preachers. We consume the words of incredible speakers, authors, and countless others whom we admire and respect; but are we looking to see if what they teach us lines up with the Word of God? Are we looking to them alone for truth? Or are we looking to our heavenly Father? Are we merely watching sermons on YouTube to discover a popular preacher's thoughts on current topics? Or are we spending time daily in the Word of God asking the Father to reveal Himself and His purposes to us through Scripture?

The intent of this book is to encourage and inspire you to not solely listen to the voices and influences of this world, but to purposefully seek out the absolute truth that we have been given in the Word of God. Either the Bible is entirely true, and as such an essential tool for our lives as Christ followers; or It does not matter at all. Either the Gospel is a transforming truth, impacting every aspect of our lives; or Christianity is meaningless. While I admittedly don't fully yet comprehend every detail of the Scriptures in my limited human understanding, as a follower of Christ, I choose to believe in the absolute truth of the Bible and fully desire to glean what God has for me to learn from it.

This is not another self-help book intended to make you feel good about yourself. I'm not going to fabricate reality with the words on these pages by claiming that I have it all figured out. The truth is that I don't. But I do know Who does and which way to direct you. I won't foolishly attempt to convince you to just do more, try harder, or simply believe in yourself with more gusto. Ultimately, the answer is Jesus, not merely doing more of what hasn't been working for you already. And I believe wholeheartedly that the Word of God is the best place for you to go to understand that fully.

May the pages ahead be a challenge for those of you who already consider yourselves followers of Christ to actually know Who God is, what Jesus did for us, and what the Word of God says. Whether you are a new believer unsure of exactly what following Jesus means or a long-time Christian desiring to grow in your spiritual maturity like Paul encourages (I Cor. 3:1-2), this book is for you. Are you ready to be challenged?

As you read through this book, my prayer is that you would choose to earnestly seek out truth, to pursue knowledge and wisdom from the Lord in His Word, and to not simply accept everything you've heard others say as absolute gospel truth, myself included. While my heart is certainly to honor my Father in everything I say and do, I am still human; and I make no claims to know everything or have it all figured out by any means. My desire is to know truth, to know the heart of my Father, to share that truth, and to share hope with a world that needs a Savior. As you walk through this book, let me encourage you to pull out your

Bible right along with it and get into God's Word. Girl, it's time to read your Bible.

CHAPTER 1

WHY READ YOUR BIBLE?

We are living in a time where tragically many people believe things simply because they like what they hear, often changing those beliefs as easily as they change socks. With so much information readily available at our fingertips on virtually every topic and from every viewpoint imaginable, it seems as though we feel free to pick and choose our beliefs based on what sounds good at the moment, perhaps now more than ever. Paul describes it perfectly for us in his letter to Timothy.

"For the time is coming when people will not endure sound teaching but having itching ears, they will accumulate for themselves teachers to suit their own passions and will turn away from listening to the truth and wander off into myths."
2 Timothy 4:3-4

Whether good or bad, right or wrong, it *feels* right to us; so we choose to accept it as truth. Or perhaps we've heard an abundance of prominent voices tell us that it's what we should believe, so we follow their lead. The argument could be made, however, that we should endeavor to be like the Bereans Paul mentions in Acts, who chose to dig deeper and search for truth in what they had heard.

> *"The brothers immediately sent Paul and Silas away by night to Berea, and when they arrived, they went into the Jewish synagogue. Now these Jews were more noble than those in Thessalonica; they received the word with all eagerness, **examining the Scriptures daily to see if these things were so**."*
> *Acts 17:10-11*

A necessity in days such as these, we absolutely must be intentional in seeking truth. Now, I don't believe that means that we need to be skeptical of everything all the time. Living in a constant state of fear and negativity is not likely to be instrumental in bringing us closer to truth. But when there are so many half-truths and even blatant lies bombarding us from all directions on countless topics, as Christ followers, don't we have an obligation to ensure that we are surrounding ourselves with truth? Shouldn't that be our foundation?

Jesus says, "I am the Way, *the Truth*, and the Life and no one comes to the Father but by Me." (John 14:6) The truth should therefore be a vital part of our lives as His followers, as He is Truth. It shouldn't be something of which we are satisfied with only knowing pieces and parts. We should wholeheartedly seek after the truth, and the Word of God is undoubtedly our best tangible resource on this earth for confidently knowing that truth.

Yes, I have my relationship with Jesus. I have the ability to pray, and I am incredibly humbled to have that intimate connection with my God. But I also acknowledge that we live in a sinful and fallen world, and our human nature can easily be an obstacle in our pursuit of truth. Our emotions and our feelings are susceptible to blend in with what we pray or what we *think* God has said to us.

How then are we able to better discern this? What keeps us from simply believing something to be true versus knowing confidently that it is? One way is simply by *knowing* what the Bible says. If something we believe to be true does not align with Scripture, then it's not of God; and we can know that with confidence. The Word of God is

9

bsolute truth, inspired by God (Ps. 33:4; Prov. 1:13; Col. 1:5; 2 Tim. 2:15; 3:16), but the only way we will be able to gain wisdom and understanding from it is by *actually* reading it.

Most believers would readily acknowledge the Bible as being a fundamental part of the armor of God (Eph. 6:10-17) without question, yet far too many of us struggle to even know what the books of the Bible are or where they are found, let alone to know anything about what is written in them. If we are not reading God's Word intentionally and often, how are we expecting to know what It says with confidence?

Perhaps you can recall the days when many Christians proudly wore their "WWJD" bracelets and would respond to life situations with that popular slogan "What Would Jesus Do?" Sadly, far too many believers have a view of what we *think* He might do based solely on the personal opinions of others. Again, we should aspire to follow the example of the Bereans that Paul spoke about in the book of Acts that searched deeper and desired to confirm what they had heard as truth.

John similarly encourages us to "test the spirits." (I John 4:1) How can we definitively *know* what Jesus would actually do if we've only heard a handful of verses or stories about Him? Wouldn't we know Him better if we actually invested time studying His life?

We sadly live in a time where our culture and even other believers are going to communicate with us topics and beliefs as truth that may not sound *quite right*. Will we choose to go along with what we hear because of the source that we received it from? Or will we compare it to God's Word? If culture contradicts something that the Word of God says, then we must remember to put our trust in what the Lord says, regardless of what may be popular at the time.

God gave us His Word as the only thing on this earth, separate creation itself, in present day physical form that we can see, we can touch, and we can learn from. Should it not then as such be an important part of our life? Do we see it as that?

We have easy access to the words that are from Jesus Himself, the words of our Creator, our heavenly Father, an incredible, perfect, amazing God. Yet how often do our Bibles simply sit on the shelf gathering dust? Day after day, month after month, possibly longer. I know that I myself have personally been guilty of such a thing and would venture to say that I'm not the only one.

v up in church. In fact, I was in church with my first Sunday after I was born. I cannot recall missing a Sunday service throughout my childhood. From a young age, I was blessed to be able to attend a private, Christian school, so I had many years of Bible study and consequently knew how to answer nearly every question about what the Bible said. Following that, I attended a Christian university. Again, there were more years of studying the Bible, reading the Bible, and completing the Bible assignments. For me, in many ways it became something to check off a to-do list. It was not about the relationship between a child and a Father, between a holy God and His creation. There was no definitive, intimate relationship there for many years.

I'm guessing some of you can relate, at least in part, to this. You have spent many months, possibly years, calling yourself a follower of Jesus Christ, yet not building that relationship and not learning what it means to grow beyond a new believer. While being fully aware of the need to repent, make Him Lord of your life, and choose to follow Him, instead you simply choose a life that looks no different than everyone else's.

I'm guilty myself of living like that. If I'm being completely honest, part of that I'm sure is because I didn't put much time or thought into knowing what it actually looked like to follow Jesus. If you read about the lives of His disciples and others who crossed paths with Him, you can clearly see the profound impact that He makes on a life. Considering this, shouldn't your life be radically transformed because of Him? Has it been?

I cannot go further without bringing your attention to the fact that knowing what the Word of God says is much more than simply reading the words. It has to be about knowing what It says, about letting those words sink in, and then studying what It means. These are not only entertaining stories in the Bible. They are things that our heavenly Father wants us to know about His nature, about who He created us to be, and about so much more. For virtually every issue, for every struggle that we have, there is wisdom that can be gained from the Word of God.

It is not about a Sunday morning feel-good story. It's not even about a daily assignment in a one-year Bible. For many of us, that has become just another thing to check off the list instead of desiring to know what God has for us in

His Word. It is a guidebook for our lives. It is not simply a collection of stories. There is *power* in the Word of God.

For the word of God is living and active,
sharper than any two-edged sword, piercing to
the division of soul and of spirit, of joints and
of marrow, and discerning the thoughts and
intentions of the heart.
Hebrews 4:12

We've got to get to the point where we no longer see it as a book that doesn't matter, that simply sits on a shelf all week gathering dust.

Recently, I was reading the history of Joshua, Caleb, and the ten other spies (Num. 13-14) when they went into Canaan and were able to see the land that God had promised them. Joshua and Caleb went back to Moses giving a report of how amazing what they had seen was, but the reports of the others were more focused on their intimidation from the giants in the land. The fear for many of them was greater than the promise.

This brought me to ponder how often in our lives we don't see all of the pieces and parts of a situation. Perhaps we focus on only one of the components, one that is daunting. Or maybe instead we're like Joshua and Caleb and our response is, "You know what? I see all of that; I'm not ignoring all of that, but my God is bigger than that circumstance. If God promised us this, then I know without a doubt that I can trust Him and that He will go before us like He said."

We can learn these truths and principles by studying the Word of God. We can learn from and be inspired reading about the life of Daniel (Dan. 6) as he chose not to bow down to another despite the threat of death and about the early life of David (I Sam. 17) as he refused to let anyone mock his God and was confident that the Lord would bring him a victory as He had shown Himself faithful many times before.

Fear does not have to control us, and we can learn this truth through the countless recollections in Scripture. We can learn the truth of Who God is. With confidence, we can know that He is more powerful and mighty than anything we face. We can be certain that we have no need to fear the things of this world. (Ps. 118:6; Prov. 29:25; Matt. 10:28; John 14:27) It is imperative for us to get into the Word to learn this and be rooted in this truth as well as many more. We have to be reading Scripture and along with it asking, "God what do You have for me to learn from this?"

If we are not intentional in our study of the Word, if we are only spending rare moments glancing at a verse that pops up on our phone occasionally or walking by a Biblical

15

quote in a decorative frame on the wall, then how do we expect to be *confident* in our knowledge of truth?

Close relationships require more than minimal to no effort in order to last. If you sincerely desire to grow closer to the Lord, you cannot expect to have an intimate relationship with Him by looking at one verse a day and that being all you ever do.

Would you consider someone to be a close friend if you simply sent each other one text a year at Easter? Would you expect to have a close relationship with your children if you never listened to them but only spoke at them? Would your marriage relationship be strong and healthy if you only said a handful of words to each other throughout the week or never sat and listened to each other?

God's Word must be a foundational part of our life if we are going to live a life following Jesus. Not simply a weekly sermon. Not simply Christian radio. Not simply books recommended from Christian authors.

I do realize the irony of that being said in a book, but the last thing I want is for this book to be your guideline for life. I absolutely do not want this to be your primary source of Biblical truth. If you believe there are statements in this book that don't align with Scripture, then please disregard what I say and take it to the Lord. Because His Word is truth. Period. All things need to pass through the filter of "Does this line up with God's Word?" If I'm going to call myself a follower of Jesus, then I need to have *that* as a guideline for my life. That needs to be my foundation of absolute truth. Now perhaps more than ever, in a world that believes there are no absolutes.

CHAPTER 2

FOLLOW YOUR HEART

Beginning at a young age, we as women often grow up watching the princess and the fairy tale movies with beautiful, strong feminine characters singing about how we should follow our heart. Ingrained in us from our youth, wherever our heart leads is the direction that we should go. Then as we grow older, it may morph into more of a "follow your passion" or perhaps "follow your dreams." Sound familiar?

The concept of following our hearts isn't anything new. In fact, Ezekiel was told by the Lord centuries ago to warn those prophesying in Israel from their own hearts and not through hearing from the Lord:

> *The word of the Lord came to me: "Son of man, prophesy against the prophets of Israel, who are prophesying, and say to those who*

> *prophesy from their own hearts: 'Hear the*
> *word of the Lord!' Thus says the Lord God,*
> *Woe to the foolish prophets who follow their*
> *own spirit, and have seen nothing!"*
> *Ezekiel 13:1-3*

The prophet Jeremiah perhaps gives us the most basic explanation for why we should *not* follow our heart. It is deceitful and as such not to be trusted.

> *The heart is deceitful above all things, and*
> *desperately sick; who can understand it?*
> *Jeremiah 17:9*

With this in mind, I'm going to submit to you that as beautiful as it may sound to follow your heart (and yes, I realize I'm probably upsetting some of your childhood memories at this very moment as you replay the songs in your head), it is not Biblical truth nor advice to which we should adhere. While I am a sucker for a good princess and brave knight story, I don't want to be deceived that my life should be based on this cliché as a foundational truth.

What else does God have to say about this though? While we can gather from Scripture that He does not instruct us to follow our heart, we can also learn that Christ did say to "follow Me." (Matt. 10:38; 16:24; Mark 8:34-35; Luke 9:23)

As His followers, we should first and foremost be following *Him* and going where He directs us.

I will be the first to acknowledge that even for longtime believers following Jesus may not be easy to do. In fact, in my experience, it rarely is. It can be incredibly challenging and may even feel uncomfortable if it's not the way we've been accustomed to living. When we choose to walk in obedience to the Lord though, it is absolutely the *best* place for us to be. He knows what is best for us. Do we trust Him enough to let him lead us? (Prov. 3:5-6)

So then, if we're called not to "follow our heart," but instead to follow Jesus, the next question would be what exactly does that mean? What does it look like to "follow Him" as He instructed? (Matt. 16:24-26; Luke 9:23-26) It's important here, as with anytime we're reading Scripture, to read beyond just those few words and see in whole what He was saying.

> Then Jesus told his disciples, "If anyone would come after me, let him **deny himself** and **take up his cross** and **follow me**. For whoever would save his life will lose it, but whoever loses his life for my sake will find it. For what will it profit a man if he gains the whole world and forfeits his soul? Or what shall a man give in

return for his soul?
Matthew 16:24-26

Luke 9:26 goes on to add to that, "For whoever is ashamed of Me and of My words, of him will the Son of Man be ashamed when He comes in His glory and the glory of the Father and of the holy angels."

When you hear the words, "follow your dreams," do your thoughts immediately go to denying selfish desires and losing your life? I would venture to say if we're being honest that not many believers have dreams that include setting aside our self in order to honor God with our lives. But I have no doubt that choosing to spend time in His Word and in prayer can not only bring us closer to Him but can also align our hearts more with His.

Psalm 37:4 says, "Delight yourself in the Lord, and He will give you the desires of your heart." I see this corresponding perfectly with Matthew 16 where we are to deny ourselves, take up our cross, and follow Him. When our hearts are lined up with the Father's, then our desires grow to be in alignment with His. When we have denied our selfish human nature and personal desires and we choose to follow Him fully, then the desires that we have are ones that are God-honoring and no longer the selfish desires that we may have had while living a life for ourselves only. So the question remains, "Do our desires align with His heart?" Or are we simply choosing to follow our own selfish desires regardless of where the Lord might be leading us to?

CHAPTER 3

ME TIME

Virtually everywhere you look, whether it's in magazines, advertisements, or books, a topic that we are constantly bombarded with is the concept of "me time," sometimes alternatively referred to as "self-care." While the idea of taking time for yourself, needing to do what makes you feel good, or focusing on yourself first so you are able to have the energy to focus on others seems like a harmless notion, if we look to Scripture, I believe we'll see that we've missed the mark on this significantly as followers of Jesus.

To put it plainly, it's not about me. And it's not about you either. Let me be clear here in that I don't say such things to imply you are not important to the Lord. Nor do I say it to make you feel less-than or unloved because neither of those are true. We do however, as Christ followers, need to look at what the Word of God says first to know with confidence if what our culture is teaching us aligns with truth. It's become easy to listen to the catchphrases and the words that sound enticing to our ears, but are we being intentional to weigh what we have been told against the Word of the Lord? Are we looking at the example that Christ set Himself?

You may be asking, "What's so wrong with 'me time'?" One could even argue, "Didn't Jesus take time away?" Yes, He absolutely did. But what did that look like for Him? While a few times Scripture mentions Jesus going to be alone (Matt. 14:13; Mark 6:31-32; Luke 9:10), the primary reason we see in Scripture that He distanced Himself from the crowds was to be in prayer undisturbed. (Matt. 14:23; Mark 1:35; 6:46; 14:32; Luke 5:15-16; 6:12; 9:18)

He chose to get away from the crowds to spend time with the Father. That is the manner in which He was refreshed. The example that we have laid out before us is to spend time with the heavenly Father to be refreshed and renewed.

I'm sorry ladies but going to get your hair and nails done is not a life necessity. Is it wrong to do those things? No, of course not. But to justify "me time" by telling people that you have to take care of yourself first in this manner so that you'll have plenty to give to others simply does not align with what the Word of God says. Scripture tells us to think of others as better than ourselves. (Phil. 2:3) It is not about me. My personal comforts and desires should not come first.

There are many examples throughout Scripture to whom we can look in order to understand this more clearly, but for me, the most powerful is the example of Christ Himself, who is the One that we are to pursue and to model our lives after. In addition to making time with the Father a priority, He put the needs of others above His own. He was blameless, yet He sacrificially gave everything of Himself for us.

I can't begin to imagine the weight of the world that He must've felt knowing what His Father was asking of Him (Luke 22:41-44), knowing full well in those moments what was coming in the days ahead. (Matt. 16:21-23; Mark 8:31-32; Luke 9:21-22) He not only endured unimaginable pain, but also suffered the anguish of feeling forsaken by His Father as He bore our sins on the cross. (Is. 53:4-5; Matt. 27:46; Gal. 3:13) Putting His own comfort aside, He did this for us.

Of all people on this earth whom we would consider had every right to make it all about Himself, He didn't choose to do that. He sacrificially gave all and put us, even as sinners (Rom. 5:8), and the will of His Father before His own personal comfort. May we fully grasp the depth of that.

Now please don't misinterpret what I've presented and assume that you should never fix your hair, grab coffee with a friend, or enjoy a day of fun with your family. Those can be wonderful blessings in our lives! But we should recognize that our thinking is flawed if after we look at what the Word of God says in regard to putting ourselves first, we continue to make our time on this earth all about us.

While I've shared why the concept of "me time" and putting yourself first does not align with Scripture, I cannot go without also acknowledging that we do, however, need rest. I truly believe that our culture has, instead of focusing on the necessary Biblical example of rest, convinced us that we need to make it only about our personal pampering.

Rest is good. I believe it could easily be argued that rest is holy. Even beginning with Creation (Gen. 2:1-3), God gave us the example to rest from our work, to be intentional to take a pause. As previously mentioned, even Jesus went away and separated Himself from the crowds and from the disciples. But He went away to be with the Father.

So why is it that we so easily find ourselves focused on "me time" for rest as opposed to "God time" for that rest? Perhaps part of this inability to recognize time with the Father as refreshment is because we have seen our time with the Lord as just a Sunday morning thing or an inside the church building experience. Maybe it's only a quick prayer before a meal or while tucking your kids in to bed and having them say their prayers that defines our connection with the Lord.

God has so much better for us, though. When we are intentional to not only spend time in the Word, but also to spend time in prayer and in His presence, it is absolutely life changing. As you make that a practice in your life, you'll see the peace that it brings to yourself, to your home, and often to your family as well.

Our time with the Lord should be our greatest priority and far too often and for far too long, myself included, it has been a last resort. It has been something we only think about when tragedies come. Or perhaps for some of us, we only think about it when life is going great; and then when everything is really hard, we just sit and wallow in our sadness and blame God that all those hard things happened.

In response to a question about his plans for the day, theologian Martin Luther pointed out the value of setting aside time with the Lord when he said,

"Work, work from early until late. In fact, I have so much to do that I shall spend the first three hours in prayer." [1]

What a great deal we have to learn in the American church when it comes to prioritizing time with the Lord in our lives.

I do believe that we also neglect to fully understand God's design for rest in our lives when we ignore the commandment to remember the Sabbath and keep it holy. (Ex. 20:8-11; Deut. 5:12-14; Ez. 20:19-20) Perhaps we've reduced it to not going to work on Sunday or maybe believing that it simply involves regular weekly church attendance. The reality is that the Sabbath is meant to be a day of rest. (Heb. 4:9-11)

Beginning as far back as Creation we can see how rest is important through God's own example to take a day of rest. (Gen. 2:3) God didn't get tired from creating everything in the universe in six days and simply need to take a big nap the next day. He set an example for us that we needed to pause, to stop our work, to set aside time for rest.

Our culture to the contrary often pushes us to go, go, go and never take pause. We have glorified busyness for far too long, and it's not difficult to see the damage that has been caused by it – parents too busy for their children, marriages damaged by misplaced priorities, overwhelming levels of personal stress, and much more.

We were intended to work hard, to serve others, and to not simply live a life being handed everything; but that does not translate to us working all day every day. Rest is good. Taking a day out of our week to set aside as a pause from our work is not only a good idea, but also a Biblical guideline. How would your life change if you traded in your "me time" for time with the Lord and Sabbath rest?

CHAPTER 4

GOD WANTS ME TO BE HAPPY

"Count it all joy, my brothers, when you meet
trials of various kinds, for you know that the
testing of your faith produces steadfastness.
And let steadfastness have its full effect, that
you may be perfect and complete, lacking in
nothing."
James 1:2-4

Did you catch that? Go back and read that verse again. James tells us *when* trials come our way to count it as an opportunity for joy. The trials and struggles *will* come, there is no question about it. The question that remains is how we will face them when they do come, not how do we avoid them. After all, isn't that how we grow?

Think back through your life over the challenges you have had to face up to now. If you're reading this, it would suggest that you've made it through every single one of those days so far, as overwhelming as they may have seemed at the time. Were there areas of growth in your life you believe you gained through those experiences? I would imagine many of us would acknowledge that we have, at least from some of life's difficulties. Through facing challenges, through stretching our faith, through learning to trust in our heavenly Father, an abundance of opportunity lies before us to strengthen us and make us more into the image of Christ. (Rom. 8:29)

Sadly, all too often it seems as though we insist on attempting to avoid any and all of life's difficulties, by any means necessary. How often do we hear the phrase "God wants me to be happy" or do we feel that as a Christian we should have an easy path set before us? Following Jesus is not easy. Jesus Himself provided a warning for those that would follow Him:

> *"If the world hates you, know that it has hated Me before it hated you. If you were of the world, the world would love you as its own; but because you are not of the world, but I chose you out of the world, therefore the world hates you…. But all these things they will do to you on account of My name, because they do not know Him who sent Me."*
> *John 15:18-19, 21*

That sure doesn't sound like happiness to me, yet that's what a life following Jesus looks like. That's what we have already been told in the Word to expect.

Let's look at the life of Paul. In one of his letters to the Corinthians, he describes an abundance of trials that he endured including countless beatings, a shipwreck, and the threat of death, among other difficulties. (2 Cor. 11:23-30) Yet he is considered to be one of the most influential voices in church history, sharing a wealth of wisdom for believers throughout generations. He understood that struggles and suffering did not equate to an absence of love from the Father, and he spoke a message not shying away from that reality. (Rom. 8:18-37) He was very straight forward about it in his letter to Timothy:

> *"Indeed, all who desire to live a godly life in Christ Jesus will be persecuted."*
> *2 Timothy 3:12*

Should we assume then, that if Scripture tells us to expect difficulty, then we are destined for a life of nothing but misery? We of course know that thought process to not be true. Although there will inevitably be times we must go through difficulties and sadness, we can nevertheless still choose joy, even in less-than-ideal circumstances. We should also be aware that we are not unseen in those seasons. (Job 28:24; Ps. 33:18; 34:15) Every tear we shed is not in vain and does not go unnoticed. (Ps. 56:8)

The unfortunate reality is that we have somehow managed to make our lives all about our comfort. When we respond with the thought process of "God wants me to be happy," it's most often a reflection of this. It may be about our complacency with our own sin or possibly a byproduct of living a lifestyle not honoring to God, but whatever it is, we're comfortable in it so we justify our choices by convincing ourselves that God *must* want us to be happy. Instead, we should be asking the question, "What does God truly want for my life?" and then pursuing holiness.

My oldest daughter has become fascinated with the life of Corrie Ten Boom in recent years and is often bringing up pieces of her story in conversation. I never cease to be amazed at the faithfulness of God in hearing about her life and have subsequently become quite inspired by the Ten Boom legacy myself. Perhaps one of my favorite recollections found in her book *The Hiding Place* is when Corrie shares of a conversation she had with her sister Betsy after they had both been sent to the Nazi concentration camps. While complaining about the flea infestation in their living quarters, Betsie encouraged her sister to be thankful for the fleas.[1] Imagine that, actually choosing to be grateful for disgusting fleas! As you can imagine, Corrie responded a bit begrudgingly in that moment, but slowly came to the profound realization of what it means to be grateful in *all* circumstances. (I Thess. 5:16-18)

Gratitude such as this can no doubt change our perspective. Instead of directing our focus on God making us happy, maybe first we should consider a heart of gratitude toward all with which we have been blessed.

Can we have joy in the midst of our circumstances? Absolutely! But joy is a choice. Happiness is an emotion. We have not been promised happiness on this earth. In fact, we have been called not to happiness, but rather to holiness. (Matt. 5:48; Rom. 12:1; 2 Cor. 7:1; 2 Tim. 1:9; Heb. 12:14) When we become intentional to see circumstances in our lives as a way to grow more into the image of Christ, it can help us to choose joy over our personal comfort and happiness.

None of this is to say we will not ever experience happiness. There will of course be blessings as well. The Lord is a good Father (Matt. 7:11; Luke 11:13), Who knows that what is best for us isn't simply a life of comfort and happiness, but rather a transformational change into the image of Christ. May we learn to keep our eyes on Jesus and off of ourselves as we choose holiness over happiness. (Matt. 6:33)

CHAPTER 5

YOU'VE GOT TO EARN IT

I'm sure most of us can easily relate to the not uncommon desire of wanting to earn the approval of others. Some of you perhaps may have felt the need to earn a parent's attention or affection from an early age. As you progress through the elementary school years and beyond in your education, there are then the added expectations to earn good grades. Later in life, it's expected that you attain a certain level of accomplishment to earn a raise or possibly a promotion at work. It's a goal to work toward that requires your very best efforts.

Throughout life, you may recognize a need to earn the respect of others elsewhere. Whether it involves friends, loved ones, co-workers, or possibly even family, you at some point may see that you have to do something to earn the love and admiration of others.

Perhaps one of the most amazing things about our relationship with Jesus is that we don't have to do anything to earn His love. There's no magical prayer that we have to say that unlocks the mystery of "When will He love me?" There are no number of good deeds we can perform that will cause Him to suddenly decide "I think I love her now."

Salvation is a free gift. (Eph 2:8-9) It was given to us. Yes, we do have a choice to accept it or not, just like any other gift, but the Bible simply says repent, believe, and you'll be saved.

> *"because, if you confess with your mouth that Jesus is Lord and believe in your heart that God raised him from the dead, you will be saved. For with the heart one believes and is justified, and with the mouth one confesses and is saved."*
> *Romans 10:9-10*

I love in Romans where Paul reminds us that Christ died for us even when we were still sinners. (Rom. 5:8) He didn't wait for us to get our messy lives sorted out and say, "Ok, *now* she's worth dying for." He didn't wait until we did all the right things and said all the right things and then thought, "I suppose *now* she's worthy enough." He paid the price to wash away our sins while we were still a mess. We did not have to earn that, which is beyond incredible.

That doesn't change after you have found Jesus. Yes, good works will follow (Eph. 4:1), but they come out of a grateful heart. (Eph. 2:8-10; James 2:17-26; Titus 1:16) We show how thankful we are for what Jesus did for us in our words and actions, but that doesn't change His love for us.

> But when the goodness and loving kindness of
> God our Savior appeared, He saved us, **not
> because of works done by us in righteousness,
> but according to His own mercy,** by the
> washing of regeneration and renewal of the
> Holy Spirit, whom He poured out on us richly
> through Jesus Christ our Savior, so that being
> justified by His grace we might become
> heirs according to the hope of eternal life.
> *Titus 3:4-7*

I'm sure there are probably many women who are reading this right now who may have struggled feeling unloved by a parent, a friend, a spouse, or another family member. Perhaps someone has only given you their approval or acceptance when you said the "right" words or behaved in a manner that they perceived to be acceptable. Believe me when I tell you that you do not have to worry about that with Jesus. We can know that with *confidence* from reading His

Word. He knew you before you were even born (Ps. 139:13-16; Jer. 1:5; Gal. 1:15), and He loved you then.

On the other side of this, if we sin and make mistakes, which we of course will do because we're human, it doesn't mean He will suddenly stop loving us. Nothing can separate us from the love of God. (Rom. 8:35-39) Even when you're the lost one. Even when think you have failed beyond comprehension, you are still loved.

I'm reminded of the infamous story of David and Bathsheba found in 2 Samuel 11-12. Here we find a great king, whom God had called, who had defended the Lord's armies and slayed the giant, who was the anointed one of Israel; yet in this setting, we see someone who has made a tremendous mess of things. He not only chose to participate in adultery, but he also plotted to have a man murdered; and yet from this, Solomon, considered by many to be the wisest and wealthiest man in all of history, was born.

If we ponder some of the colossal mistakes we've made in our life, maybe we wouldn't put them on quite the same scale, but I'd imagine many of us could reflect on a mess that we would think, "There is no way that I can recover from this one." Perhaps at some point in your life you've wondered if something you'd done was so big it couldn't possibly be forgiven. And yet looking at Acts 13:22, we can see how special David was to the Lord. In fact, the lineage of Christ even came through David. God still used him, even after this disaster of a situation that we would possibly see as unforgivable.

That said, our life's choices are not without consequence. David still had painful consequences to face after what he had done. (2 Sam. 12:10-19) Does this mean, though, that God doesn't love us? Does that mean that He's given up on us? That there's no hope? Absolutely not! David acknowledged his sin (2 Sam. 12:13), repented of it (Ps. 51), and was restored in his relationship with the Lord.

Jesus tells the story of the prodigal son in Luke 15:11-32. It isn't difficult to visualize the father standing there watching and waiting for the son to return. Let me challenge you to take the time to read through that portion of Scripture from the eyes of the wayward child. This powerful story of love and forgiveness paints a beautiful picture of the depths of our Father's love for us.

Along the same lines, we can read the parable of the lost sheep in Matthew 18 & Luke 15. What a profound realization of our value in the eyes of the Shepherd, who believes the lost one is not too far gone. Personally, I have many times been overwhelmed by the mercy of the Father when I recognized that at some point in my life, *I* was the lost sheep.

If you gather nothing else from this book but this, know that you are loved wholly and deeply by your Creator. Not because of anything you have or have not done, but because you are His creation and He desires to have a relationship with you. You do not have to earn His love. He loved you enough to send His Son as a sacrifice so that you do not have to be eternally separated from Him. But He also loves you enough to not leave you where you are. He loves you enough to call you to more.

You do not need to do anything to earn His love. And just like in the parable of the prodigal son, it does not matter how far you've run or how horribly you believe you've messed up. He is waiting with open arms for you to come back and receive the love that He has for you. None of this is anything we have earned – it is through the Father's love and His Son Jesus' sacrifice alone that we can be called a child of God.

CHAPTER 6

JUDGE NOT

Perhaps one of the most misused and misunderstood portions of Scripture, Matthew 7 shares with us Jesus' words regarding our hearts in the judgment of others.

> *"Judge not, that you be not judged. For with the judgment you pronounce you will be judged, and with the measure you use it will be measured to you. Why do you see the speck that is in your brother's eye, but do not notice the log that is in your own eye? Or how can you say to your brother, 'Let me take the speck out of your eye,' when there is the log in your own eye? You hypocrite, first take the log out of your own eye, and **then you will see clearly to take the speck out of your brother's eye**."*
> *Matthew 7:1-5*
> *(also found in Luke 6:37-42)*

A common phrase heard among both Christians and non is "judge not," but frankly, it's not the whole picture.

When this portion of Scripture is read in its full context, you can see that you will be judged in the same manner that you judge others, a meaning much different than the aforementioned condensed version that most of us have heard and perhaps even believed.

Here we can also find an admonition from Jesus to "get the plank out of our own eye" before bringing up the little speck in someone else's eye. (Matt. 7:3-5) Basically, don't point out the sins in someone else's life before making sure your heart is right. While we've been convinced that we should mind our own business regarding the affairs of others, we can actually read throughout Scripture that as believers we are expected to keep each other accountable. (John 7:24; Rom. 14; I Cor. 4:5; Gal. 6:1; 2 Tim. 4:2)

God calls us to community as Christ followers for a reason. If I am somehow not living a life that is honoring to God, then I should be willing to allow another believer to lovingly bring to my attention something that may be in my life that may be out of alignment Biblically. Yet many of us have not allowed those types of relationships in our lives as we should.

"Iron sharpens iron, and one man sharpens
another."
Proverbs 27:17

We're not intended to live life on our own. The enemy is on the prowl looking to destroy us (I Pet. 5:8), and as such it is vital that we surround ourselves with other believers living life transparently so they can lovingly and Biblically challenge and encourage us. We *should* be keeping each other accountable.

Being a part of community is not solely so we can enjoy some potlucks together and then live our own separate lives. Of course it also doesn't mean I need to criticize everyone I encounter simply to tell them everything I feel they're doing that's wrong (Rom. 14:10-23); but if I love these people and I know that they want to honor God with their lives, then I must recognize that it's not loving for me at all to watch them walk in sin, to do things directly against what the Lord asks of us, and then not say or do anything about it - especially in the name of love. (I Cor. 13:6)

In a similar respect, another incredibly damaging philosophy permitted in the body of believers is that of "you do you." I have known far too many believers who knowingly observe another believer who has wandered away from their relationship with God, and their response is that they don't want to get involved or that it's not their business. We are called as the body of Christ to encourage and exhort one another, to speak truth into other believers' lives. We are members of one body (Rom. 12:5; I Cor. 12:12-31), and as such we were not intended to live our lives in solitude and without connection.

Are we more concerned about our personal comfort and not having to go through an awkward situation, or are we prioritizing our concern with someone who is choosing to walk away from following Christ? What does the Word of God say about these things? It is imperative that we read our Bibles to confidently know the answers. We must stop responding the way we've always heard. We must stop stepping away from those things that are challenging or difficult. We need to be able to speak truth!

Would it be considered loving to watch as someone is running toward the edge of a cliff all the while doing nothing to stop them due to fear of offending or upsetting them? This may seem a bit dramatic, but if we truly grasped the gravity of sin in our lives and see it how the Father sees it, then perhaps we should consider it is a more serious matter than we may make it to be in our lives.

We must also recognize that we cannot change the hearts of others. God is the One Who changes hearts. (I Sam. 10:9; Ez. 11:19; 36:26; Ps. 51:10; I Cor. 3:6-7) But if we see another believer living a life far from the Lord, then as a fellow believer, we do have a responsibility to lift them up, to encourage them, and to speak Biblical truth into their lives. (Zech. 8:16; Eph. 4:11-16; 4:25)

> *My brothers, if anyone among you wanders*
> *from the truth and someone brings him*
> *back, let him know that whoever brings back a*
> *sinner from his wandering will save his soul*
> *from death and will cover a multitude of sins.*
> *James 5:19-20*

I cannot cause them to make the right choices, but if I watch someone doing something that I know to be sin, if I'm watching someone live a life that separates them from the Father, then shame on me for being so concerned about my comfort and myself that I do not lovingly speak truth into their lives. Jesus Himself spoke the truth, and sometimes it offended people; but He knew it needed to be spoken. (Matt. 13:53-58; 15:1-20; Mark 2:5-7; 11:15-19; 14:53-65; John 8:57-59) Are we motivated by that same love Jesus had to see others restored to the Father in our conversations?

49

It is important to note that there is a difference between holding other believers accountable and simply being judgmental. Is what we're saying coming from a critical spirit? Or are our intentions to restore and build up those in the church? The goal should always be restoration. Scripture calls us to build up the church (Eph. 4:1-32), to confront sin with humbleness (Gal. 6:1-6), and to seek reconciliation.

It's also important to point out here that when we bring up the discussion of judging others, Biblically we are called to encourage, uplift, and speak truth to those in the church. It is not our job however to judge those outside of the church. (I Cor. 5:12-13) We are to go and share the Good News (Mark 16:15), but we are not instructed to go and tell the entire world that we're better than them, which is often how Christians come across.

Additionally, our judgment should not be based on outward appearances or assumptions. Are the matters we believe need to be addressed ones of our own personal preference or are they actually in violation of the Word of God? In our judgment, are we making assumptions about the intentions of others? Are we simply criticizing for the sake of being critical? Are we gossiping and discussing the topic? Or in our judgement, are our hearts pure and desiring to see other believers restored back to right relationship with the Father.

God knows the heart. He also instructs us to hold each other accountable for the purpose of restoration. (Matt. 18:15-20) May our judgment of one another as believers be pure in heart and with the intentions of grace, restoration, and repentance as the Word of God directs. (James 1:9; James 5:16; I Cor. 15:1-2)

CHAPTER 7

YOU ARE ENOUGH

*For if anyone thinks he is something, when he
is nothing, he deceives himself.*
Galatians 6:3

Recently, I was walking through a store and noticed a home decor wall hanging with the words "YOU ARE ENOUGH" in big bold letters. I looked at it and immediately thought, "No, I am not." Please understand that I genuinely don't have self-esteem issues. On the contrary, I am boldly confident in who I am as a child of God, and this is not an area I tend to struggle with personally.

It seems as though society has in some ways overcompensated for the fact that people are increasingly depressed, sad, and lonely in our world; so we've tried to inspire them with seemingly encouraging, although somewhat shallow, phrases such as this. But the reality is that without Jesus, frankly, I'm *not* enough. None of us are.

*"Remain in me, as I also remain in you. No branch can bear fruit by itself; it must remain in the vine. Neither can you bear fruit unless you remain in Me. I am the vine; you are the branches. If you remain in Me and I in you, you will bear much fruit; **apart from Me you can do nothing**."*
John 15:4-5

Now I'm not going to convince you to feel sorry for me in my dramatic revelation that I'm just a horrible, worthless sinner; although yes, I am human and do sin. But I will implore you to consider that perhaps we have come to use these catch phrases in place of searching for the truth and discovering the root of the real issue.

Someone telling me I am "enough," when I am not, is not sincerely helpful. In fact, it can often times actually have the opposite effect and be quite damaging. While words are incredibly powerful, they do not have the ability to directly change reality. It doesn't matter how many times your mom told you that you had the voice of an angel. If you can't carry a tune, then a career in singing isn't looking too promising regardless of your glowing recommendation from home. Opinion simply does not equate to truth.

As women, it is sadly not uncommon for us to face self-esteem issues or to struggle with feelings that we are "enough." Due to life circumstances, I have in recent years personally come to recognize that what matters most is what God says about me – not solely what others' opinions are of me are. Getting into the Word of God is the foundation of what has brought me to this deep-rooted understanding.

We need Jesus. Period. And without Him, God's Word clearly tells us that *we* are not enough. With Him? Now that's another story.

> *"I can do all things **through Him** who strengthens me."*
> *Philippians 4:13*

Notice here in Philippians that Paul does not say, "I can do all things," and stop there. We are not worthy. Jesus does change that for us, and for that I am forever immensely grateful. But our abilities, our strengths, our "enough" comes from Him. So perhaps we should at least consider that it shouldn't be said simply, "You are enough," but instead, "With Christ, you are enough."

A friend and I recently authored a Biblical study on identity for women, a much-needed deep dive into what the Bible says about who we are as followers of Christ. I think often we get in our own heads, especially as women, and focus on all of the things that we're not. Perhaps even beyond our thoughts of not being good enough, we have found our identity in ourselves *solely* as a mom, as a wife, as a coworker, or as a daughter. It's so important though that we get back into the Word of God and see what He says. That is not *who* we are. Maybe it's a part of what we do while we're on this earth, but first and foremost the core of our identity is as a child of God.

If you have made Jesus Lord of your life, then you are a daughter of the Most High God, and nothing can take that from you. No one can take that from you. So many times, life circumstances will knock us down and if our identity is rooted in anything apart from Him, then we are setting ourselves up for a future of disappointment.

It's not hard to envision a situation where your identity is in your career and when you unexpectedly lose your job due to unforeseen reasons you're easily sent into a downward spiral. But when you find your true identity in Christ and confidently know who you are and what the Word of God says about you, then that cannot be taken away from you regardless of circumstances that may surround you.

What *does* Scripture say about who you truly are then? The Bible says you are God's child. (I John 3:1) The Bible says you are His masterpiece. (Eph. 2:10) The Bible says you are not alone. (Matt. 28:20) How many of us need to be reminded of that truth on occasion? The Bible says you are part of a family. (Eph. 2:19-22) For those of us that may struggle with family relationships, it is incredible to know that because of Christ's sacrifice for us we are now able to be a part of a loving family. The Bible says you are valuable. (Luke 12:6-7) The Bible says you are more than a conqueror (Rom. 8:37), you are a new creation (2 Cor. 5:17), and you are chosen. (John 15:16) May we strive to be women of the Word who choose to continue to search for Biblical truth as it relates to our identity.

While I will admit that I'm personally not a fan of the "you are enough" motto or merch that supports it, I do know exactly who I am. I am a child of God most importantly; and no matter what circumstances are thrown my way in my life, that cannot be changed. I am a daughter of the King. And that means something pretty incredible, much more to me than "you are enough."

CHAPTER 8

THE ROOT OF ALL EVIL

Not long ago, my family was in a church service where a guest speaker brought up in his sermon the notion that it was sinful to be wealthy. Honestly, I was bothered in the moment knowing how it was presented was not Biblical, but I vocalized nothing to my family sitting in the service with me. Upon getting in our vehicle after the service, however, one of my kids immediately asked me why the preacher was saying money was bad when the Bible doesn't say that it is.

It is a great tragedy when the church portrays concepts such as these contrary to the actual Word of God. This is also an excellent example again of why we need to read the Bible for ourselves and not be complacent in allowing ourselves to being spoon-fed, regardless of the well-intentioned source. For years, I have pointed my children to

Scripture regarding truth and encouraged them to read the Bible for themselves from an early age. I want them to know what God says, not simply what others tell them He might have said.

Unfortunately, it seems as though we have somehow put a platform on poverty in the church. It's almost as if when you're a Christian, you're "supposed" to be poor and have nothing. We've all likely heard reference to I Timothy 6:10 and money being described as the "root of all evil," and perhaps that's where this ideology is derived from, but there are well over 2,000 verses about wealth and money in the Bible. Let's look a bit more closely at what God's Word has to say on this topic.

Let's just start with those verses written in the first letter to Timothy that we've likely all heard reference to:

> *"For the love of money is a root of all kinds of evils. It is through this craving that some have wandered away from the faith and pierced themselves with many pangs."*
> *I Timothy 6:10*

If we look at the entirety of what the Scripture says here, we can see that it is not actually talking about the money being evil or even money being the root of all evil. It speaks to the love of money itself and being a cause of all kinds of evils. It doesn't specifically acknowledge that *all* evil comes from that, and it definitely does not say that money itself is evil.

Another common portion of Scripture that may come to mind when discussing wealth would be that of the rich young ruler. (Matt. 19:16-22; Mark 10:17-27; Luke 18:18-23) In this particular encounter with Jesus, a very wealthy man asked what he must do to have eternal life. Jesus responded by reminding him to keep the commandments, and when the man replied that he had, followed it up by challenging him to give away all that he had. For this man, his love for money was greater than his desire to love and follow Jesus. Consequently, he walked away sad. (Matt.19:22)

Perhaps this is where we have derived our preconceived notion that money is in and of itself bad as this is also the same portion of Scripture in which Jesus referred to it being "easier for a camel to go through the eye of a needle than for a rich person to enter the kingdom of God." (Matt. 19:24) When read in its entirety, however, we can clearly see that this man put his wealth above everything else, and *that* was the heart of the matter Jesus was addressing.

Yes, money can be a stumbling block just as many other things in this world can be – popularity, possessions, personal comfort. Any of these can be inappropriately prioritized in our lives if we allow. The real question we should be asking is "Where does my heart lie in the matter?"

Would you be willing to give up everything if Jesus asked that of you? I imagine that the struggle to do so may be greater for those who have built up their wealth and allowed it to become their source of identity in some way, as it was for the rich young ruler. If, however, we instead acknowledge that all we possess is not ours to begin with, then the answer to that question may be a bit more easy to come by. (Ex. 19:5; Job 41:11; Ps. 24:1)

Let's look at some other examples in Scripture of people who were wealthy and see what the Bible has to say about them. In Genesis, we can read about Abraham who was rich in gold, silver, and cattle. (Gen. 13:2; 24:35) His wealth in today's currency would be comparable to a multibillion-dollar business. And yet in Genesis 21, we can see how God continued to bless him. We see no indication through this that God was disappointed in Abraham living with abundance, nor did He think Abraham had so much that it needed to be taken away from him. In Genesis 13:6, we even read that Abraham had so much that he and Lot needed to separate from each other as there was not enough room in the land for them any longer. He was a very wealthy man, yet in James 2:23, he is referred to as a friend of God still.

Looking further into Genesis we find Isaac, Abraham's son, of whom we learn "was able to plant and harvest one hundred times more than others." (Gen. 26:12) Here we can see that the blessings from the Lord continued onto the next generation in that Isaac was also a man of affluence. Further on in the same chapter, you can learn that Isaac continued to receive even *more* blessings.

We read all throughout Scripture of "the God of Abraham, Isaac, and Jacob." For the Israelites, these men were considered pillars of their faith, highly respected and known for their devotion to the Lord; yet we also see an abundance of financial blessings in their lives. The wealth and abundance that they had was not portrayed in their lives as an evil thing. God loved them and allowed these blessings in their lives and those of their families.

As we look further into the Old Testament, we can learn about the life of Job. While most of us are likely familiar with the tragedies that befell Job in his life, how many of us are familiar with his abundant wealth?

Job is introduced to us in Scripture as the wealthiest in the land. (Job 1:3) He was extremely wealthy and then he went through a string of tragedies losing virtually everything – his livestock, seven sons, and three daughters, among other possessions; yet in Job 42:10 we can see that after he had gone through all of the testing and the trials, the Lord restored even more than he had before. He was given riches that surpassed all that he had previously owned. We can see here that the abundance from the Lord was not something to be maligned. God can and does bless those that serve and love Him. Job is just one more Biblical example of this.

One of the wealthiest men in all of existence is talked about in I Kings. The vast wealth of Solomon is described in detail in I Kings 10:14-25. Arguably also the *wisest* man who ever lived (I Kings 4:29-34), Solomon knew what to do with his money. His wealth in today's money would be around the equivalent of two trillion dollars[1] (far richer than Elon Musk, Jeff Bezos, Bill Gates, Mark Zuckerburg, and Warren Buffet combined.)[2] Yet nothing in Scripture tells us that Solomon owning these possessions was sinful in nature.

We also learn from Solomon in his vast wisdom some of the Biblical principles about money. Labor brings profit. (Prov. 14:23) Diligence brings wealth. (Prov. 10:4) You gain by honesty. (Prov. 13:11) Honor the Lord with your possessions. (Prov. 3:9-10)

These portions of Scripture help to show us a Biblical view of wealth. God-honoring wealth does not come from stealing or swindling others out of their money. It comes from hard, honest, diligent work and through being honest in our business practices.

Additionally, the parable of the talents in the New Testament provides for us yet another example of Biblical stewardship. (Matt. 25:14-30; Luke 19:11-27) What are we doing with what we have been given? Whether it be money, resources, or any number of blessings, should we not choose to be good keepers of what we have been entrusted with on this earth? How would our lives look different if we actually applied these principles?

Am I saying that God wants all of us to have mansions, jewelry boxes full of diamonds, private jets, and the latest fashions? That's not at all what I'm implying here. Do we realize as His followers, though, how much more we could do for the kingdom of God if we did have the resources in abundance with which to spread the gospel and help others in need? Or do we perhaps fear the thought of growing a business or charging for goods or services as if somehow poverty makes us holier?

No doubt there are times that God does want to show Himself mightily as our Provider. I can recall situations in my own life where I wondered where the money for something was going to come from when it suddenly showed up. God gets *all* the glory for that. But that does not mean that God cannot also work in ways that He chooses to bless my finances or your finances so that we can use that to bless others in turn.

For me, the bottom line is realizing it is not my money to begin with - whatever I have, I hold loosely. If God calls me to give all that I have and follow His lead trusting Him completely, then my desire to be obedient to Him should be greater than my desire to hold onto my wealth.

While we can acknowledge that money may be a stumbling block for some, we must recognize that does not negate the fact that God can and does use it as a tool for His kingdom and His glory. Let me challenge you to dig further into the Word of God, into the thousands of verses related to money and wealth, and see what else the Lord would have for you to learn from this.

Are you living a life unable to help those in need because you're struggling to pay your own bills? Are you unable to leave everything you have and go where God calls you to go to share the gospel because your possessions are of greater value to you than a life sold out for Him? Are you fearful of stepping out in faith to look for more opportunities to serve others and in turn grow your finances because you believe having wealth is sinful? These are questions only you can answer, but allow me to challenge you to balance your possible preconceived beliefs about wealth and money in light of the Word of God.

CHAPTER 9

LOVE IS LOVE

"Love is patient and kind; love does not envy or boast; it is not arrogant or rude. It does not insist on its own way; it is not irritable or resentful; it does not rejoice at wrongdoing but rejoices with the truth. Love bears all things, believes all things, hopes all things, endures all things. Love never ends...."
I Corinthians 13:4-8a

As followers of Jesus, we have the precious gift of the Word of God to help us to understand what our heavenly Father wants us to know. It should be our foundation of truth if we consider ourselves to be Christ followers. With that in mind, these verses contain the most powerful and thorough explanation imaginable of what love is. The Bible also says that God is love. (I John 4:8) So the phrase "love is love" is simply not accurate in its intent of definition. The Bible tells us exactly what love is. Are we willing to earnestly study

God's Word to gain wisdom and understanding on these and other hot topics that the world around us may disagree with?

The current culture in and of the American church unfortunately seems to skim over verse six in the love chapter of Corinthians where it says, "love does not delight in evil but rejoices with the truth." Somehow the explanation of "love your neighbor" has been inaccurately translated into "be nice and accept everything everyone does," which is absolutely not Biblical.

Jesus was a pretty in-your-face kind of guy at times. Telling Peter, "get behind me Satan," (Matt. 16:23; Mark 8:33) and calling the Pharisees a "brood of vipers" (Matt. 12:34; Matt. 23:33) sure doesn't sound like "Mr. Nice Guy" to me. I imagine we are all likely familiar with the infamous flipping of the tables in the temple as well. (Matt. 21:12-13; Mark 11:15-18)

While Jesus was full of mercy and grace, He also did not have a tolerance for lies and evil. And as believers, neither should we. Clearly Jesus was perfect; and we are not, nor will we be while on this earth. But we can follow His example by learning who He was and what He did. We can be diligent in studying the Word of God and seeing what the

Bible has to say, not what the popular thought of the day is, whether taught in church circles or not.

Does God want us to love other people? Absolutely! It's one of the two greatest commandments of which He spoke. (Matt. 22:36-40; Mark 12:28-34) But loving our neighbor does not mean ignoring the sin that they're in. Upon Jesus meeting the Samaritan woman at the well (John 4:1-26), He showed love and kindness to her, but He did not ignore the circumstances of her life nor condone her lifestyle. He spoke truth over it.

When people met Jesus, they were changed. Is that what happens when people are around us? I'm not telling you to go and get picket signs and tell people how evil and wrong they are. But are we watching other believers around us living their lives in sin and telling them that it's ok? Allowing them to be comfortable in it? When Jesus returns, I don't want to be held accountable for saying I know that they were living in sin and neither said nor did anything because I simply wanted to be nice to them and preferred not to feel uncomfortable.

God's definition of love is different than ours, and it shouldn't be that way. We tell others to "just love people."

Jesus loved people, and He also called them out when they were living in sin *because* of that love.

In Paul's first letter to the Corinthians, he talks about a man among the body of believers who was living in sin, knew that he was living in sin, yet he was still joining the believers in assembly. Paul basically tells those in the church in Corinth to kick him out of the body of believers and let him hit rock bottom so he can find his way back to Jesus. (I Cor. 5) Our current church culture in America most likely wouldn't consider that to be loving. However, that *is* loving, as the intent in doing so was "so that his spirit may be saved in the day of the Lord." (I Cor. 5:5)

Jesus loves all people, but He cannot and does not love all things. When sin, any sin, separates us from God, He does not ignore, protect, or promote it; and neither should we as His followers. Romans 1:24-27 is very clear that homosexuality is a sin, and yes, we all sin and fall short of God's glory. But we also need to acknowledge sin as sin and God's Word as truth if we are going to claim Him as Lord of our lives.

"Or do you not know that the unrighteous will not inherit the kingdom of God? Do not be deceived: neither the sexually immoral, nor

*idolaters, nor adulterers, **nor men who
practice homosexuality**, nor thieves, nor the
greedy, nor drunkards, nor revilers, nor
swindlers will inherit the kingdom of God."*
I Corinthians 6:9-10

According to the Word of God, those living a homosexual lifestyle from which is derived the statement of "love is love" cannot enter the kingdom of Heaven. It grieves me to know that churches and believers are turning a blind eye to this truth, possibly even believing that their acceptance is an act of love. While our responses toward those living a sexually immoral lifestyle should be different concerning those inside versus those outside of the church body (I Cor. 5:9-13), we still must not be blind to the truth in our acceptance of sin disguised in the name of love.

Are we deriving our definition of love from culture or from God's Word? If we are to be known by our love (John 13:35), shouldn't our love be reflective of the Father's love and defined by Him alone?

CHAPTER 10

LIVE YOUR BEST LIFE NOW

You may be familiar with the popular sermon illustration of the pastor holding a long rope, often running the distance of the room. At the end of that rope that he's holding is a small portion that's covered with a piece of tape or some sort of marking. He then compares the little tape at the end to the equivalent of our lifetime, the time that we've been given here on this earth. The rest of the rope that extends as far as the eye can see in some cases is eternity. In light of such a comparison, what a tragedy it is that we spend so much of our time focused on that almost insignificant part of our lives in comparison to eternity and our comfort here.

No doubt it is our human nature that is at the root of at least some of this - to only think in the here and now. We are finite beings and God is not, so our concept of time is understandably unique from His.

"yet you do not know what tomorrow will bring. What is your life? For you are a mist that appears for a little time and then vanishes."
James 4:14

God's Word encourages us to live with eternity in mind. (I Cor.7:29-31; 2 Cor. 4:16-17; I Pet. 4:7-11) As such, shouldn't we perhaps consider more than we do what is after this?

Does this mean that we ignore the life that we have here? No. Does that mean that we must deny ourselves enjoyment of anything while we're on this earth? Of course not. But are we focused on the best parts being right now? Are we only serving our selfish, human nature in an attempt for our best life to be now, or are we *more* focused on eternal life with our heavenly Father?

How would our lives look different if we were focused not primarily on the here and now but were intentionally focused instead on eternity? How would it impact our time and our resources? How would it impact our conversations and relationships?

I want my life to honor God; and while sometimes that may mean there are some incredibly joyous occasions, that's also going to mean there will sometimes be really difficult moments. We've already discussed how God can and does use those moments to strengthen and to grow us.

I want to become more like Christ, and in order for that to happen, things are not always going to be comfortable, exciting, or without struggle. I believe many of us would acknowledge that if we ask God to give us patience, then often He gives us plenty of opportunities to exercise patience. The same is true for many other areas of growth as well. The struggles are what produce the endurance, so why do we strive so intently to have everything be "perfect" while we live life on this earth?

> *"as we look not to the things that are seen but to the things that are unseen. For the things that are seen are transient, but the things that are unseen are eternal."*
> 2 Corinthians 4:18

This is not the best that there is. The absolute best is still ahead for those who have made Jesus Lord of their lives. The best is not intended to be now. I don't know about you, but I don't *want* my best life to be now. I want to honor my

God now, regardless of what that looks like in my daily life, so that I can spend eternity with Him and have *that* be the best part. May we be challenged by God's Word to live with eternity in mind and allow our days to be molded by that.

CHAPTER 11

HOSPITAL FOR SINNERS

If I were to survey believers in the American church with the question "Do non-believers belong in worship services?" there is no doubt in my mind that the response would be overwhelmingly affirmative. The question I present to you once again though is if this a Biblically accurate response or simply one that we have become accustomed to through our cultural norms. A profound discussion crossed my path recently that inspired me to dig deeper on this topic personally: If you were asked to describe church using only Scripture, what would you say?

In the American church in particular, we seem to have decided that the role of pastors and those in church leadership is to save those who are lost. We're told to bring our unsaved friends and family with us to a service on Easter. Campaigns are designed and promoted to convince us to invite our neighbors or coworkers to come to church with us so they can hear the Gospel.

I'm going to challenge you once again to put aside your preconceived notions on this topic and again get back to the basics of God's Word. Biblically speaking, first and foremost, the church is not a building. I imagine most believers would probably agree with that statement, although in our conversations we still do primarily think of it in that way. What we may miss in our perception of church, however, is that it is not designed for non-believers. *Nelson's Bible Dictionary* describes church as "a local assembly of believers as well as the redeemed of all the ages who follow Jesus Christ as Savior and Lord."[1]

Scripture supports the argument that believers are supposed to *be* the church. Believers are the ones that are responsible for leading people to Jesus. And only believers are the ones that are a part of the body of Christ.

You have probably heard the quote "a church is a hospital for sinners, not a museum for saints," but is the church *really* a hospital for sinners? This is one of those things that sounds good, but again, I'm going to refer you to what I've been saying throughout this whole book. Girl, read your Bible. Does this encouraging, positive-sounding quote line up with the truth of the Word of God?

Some would argue "it's the sick who need a doctor," (Matt. 9:10-13) so therefore the church is a hospital for the lost. I'm not disagreeing with the fact that the broken, sick, and lost are in need of a Savior. But I am saying that bringing them to a church building to be saved is not the example we have set for us in Scripture. Jesus didn't wait for non-believers to show up at the temple. That's not likely somewhere they would've been found. As he was traveling and living his life, He would heal, He would preach, and He would send the disciples out to reach people wherever they were.

We don't have to have our lives all figured out before we meet Jesus. He does meet people where they are, but He does not leave them there; He leaves them changed. He also does not desire for them to become immersed in the body of believers as they are.

In Paul's first letter to the Corinthians, you may recall reading about the man in the church body who was aware of the sin he was living in, yet was still choosing it. What did Paul instruct in this circumstance? He said that he should be separated from the body. (I Cor. 5)

We must not allow sin and the complacency of such to settle in among the gathering of believers. We are to be set apart, to be in the world but not of it. (John 17:14-16) When you take the time to be intentional in reading God's Word, you can learn the depths of what this truly means.

In the Old Testament, we can learn how God wanted His chosen people, the Israelites, set apart; and whenever they went to a new place, He wanted them to completely rid that area of the people, possessions, and gods that were there, the things that would draw them away from Him. In the New Testament, we see the same thing. (John 15:19; Rom. 12:2; 1 Cor. 6:9-11; 2 Cor. 5:17; 6:14-18) If there are those that are going to be pulling you away from following Christ, they should not have a place of influence in your life, nor do they belong in fellowship with believers as part of the body of Christ.

*"Your boasting is not good. Do you not know that **a little leaven leavens the whole lump**? Cleanse out the old leaven that you may be a new lump, as you really are unleavened. For Christ, our Passover lamb, has been sacrificed. Let us therefore celebrate the festival, not with the old leaven, the leaven of malice and evil, but with the unleavened bread of sincerity and*

truth."
I Corinthians 5:6-8

Please don't misunderstand what I'm describing as some "high and mighty" social club. The point remains, though, that you cannot have believers being discipled and getting deep into the Word of God, growing beyond the newborn milk spoken of in Hebrews (5:11-14) when there are unbelievers in their midst. You cannot mix darkness and light. (2 Cor. 6:14)

While we can glean from Scripture that the church body is intended for believers, we should also acknowledge that no one should be turned away who wanders in. (I Cor. 14:22-25) Non-believers of course should be welcomed and loved, but there is no basis Biblically for the gathering of the church to be designed *for* them.

It also cannot be forgotten that we should of course be praying for those who have not yet come to know Christ as Lord of their lives, and we are to love them where they are. We also need to be speaking Biblical truth to them as the Lord directs, but that does not mean that they are to be a part of the church as unbelievers. This is the example Jesus Himself set before us, along with those of the disciples, Paul, and others.

83

*"You were running well. Who hindered
you from obeying the truth? This
persuasion is not from him who calls
you. A little leaven leavens the whole
lump."*
Galatians 5:7-9

I believe that our churches in America have suffered greatly from this "leaven growth," due at least in part to pastors and those in church leadership not acknowledging this Biblical truth with their congregations. Admittedly, I cannot deny that in our current American culture, this would be quite a challenging undertaking. For years, though, pastors have taught us to invite non-Christians to church and consequently have been allowing members to believe they are fulfilling the Great Commission, going out into all the world, making disciples, and preaching the good news; when in reality, we're just passing the buck.

We justify the denial of our personal God-directed responsibility when we "invite someone," all the while waiting for someone else to share the good news with them. When you're inviting your unsaved coworkers or neighbors to come to a Sunday service with you, you're implying that the only place one can receive forgiveness or be in the presence of God is within the four walls of a designated building. Countless persecuted Christians around the world would most definitely acknowledge this as a grave misconception. How many more believers might there be if we actually lived out the Great Commission and didn't choose to abdicate our responsibilities, passing the buck onto church staff or others?

Contrary to the Word of God, instead of a meeting of believers being a place of sharpening and encouragement where we can inspire each other to grow closer to the Lord, we have tragically allowed it to be a place where those who gather feel comfortable in their sin. More often than not, there is little to no accountability among believers, no perceived need for repentance, or even the acknowledgment of a need for a Savior because however we are living is just fine. We live under the guise that we can all, believers and non, come together for a few moments a week, hear a nice story from someone on a stage, then go home and continue to live life as we please. I believe we are called to something greater, to something much more than that with which we have settled.

The church in America is weak and broken, in desperate need of a Savior, regardless of how many years the physical doors of a building have been open on a Sunday morning. My fear is that many believe that they are following Jesus and claim to be Christians but know nothing about Who He is or if He is even Lord of their lives. (Matt 7:21-23; Heb. 6; 10) I do not naively believe this is exclusive to America, but for the majority of the history of our nation we have not faced true persecution for our faith and have consequently grown complacent. We must get back to the basics of reading God's Word to learn Who our God is and what it means to follow Him.

So what should our church gatherings look like then? Perhaps we should at least consider what the behaviors of the early church were (Acts 2:42; 46-47) rather than simply relying on modern tradition for our inspiration. May we all learn to seek God's Word more on topics such as these, regardless of what we have grown up believing or what we have been told.

CHAPTER 12

WHAT'S NEXT?

*"All Scripture is breathed out by God and
profitable for teaching, for reproof, for
correction, and for training in righteousness,"*
2 Timothy 3:16

While this book has hopefully brought to your attention a need to search for Biblical truth beyond simply familiar things that you have heard, you may still be wondering, "What now?" I would be remiss to not share what impact this should have on your life.

The Word of God is not just words on a page that we read. It serves a purpose. We should be doers of the Word, not simply hearers. (James 1:22) So while the focus may have seemingly been to simply read your Bible, it cannot be a matter of merely looking at the words on the pages and then going back to life as usual. True understanding cannot help but bring notable change.

*"Do not be conformed to this world, but **be
transformed by the renewal of your mind,**
that by testing you may discern what is the will
of God, what is good and acceptable and
perfect."*
Romans 12:2

Just because we may hear things that are popular or that sound enticing, as children of God we are to be *transformed* by the renewing of our minds. We must be spending time with the Lord, both in prayer and in the reading of God's Word, learning from what we read and growing in our relationship with Him.

I challenge you to not simply accept things that you have always thought to be true, especially things that are common in the culture of today. Just because it is widely held in society or even taught in the church as true does not make it Biblical truth.

It is imperative for us to get into the Word to spend time learning about what the Bible says. We like to hear what makes us feel good; we like to hear what makes us proud of ourselves and that justifies our behavior. (2 Tim. 4:3) It's part of our selfish human nature.

Contrary to that human nature is forgiving our enemies. We are not innately inclined to forgive repeatedly as we should even if we do choose to forgive. (Matt. 18:22) Embracing correction does not come naturally for us, but is a necessary part of our lives as believers. (Prov.11:14; 15:5; I Cor. 10:12) And again contrary to our natural tendency is accepting the concept of being still and trusting the Lord. (Ex. 14:14; Ps. 37:7; 62:5-6; Is. 40:31) We should look different than the world around us, should we not? Do we stand out as a light in the darkness in such a way? (Matt. 5:14-16)

Paul encouraged Timothy to be ready in and out of season. (2 Tim. 4:2) Should we not heed that same advice? No matter what the world looks like around us, we need to know what God's Word says and not assume that we have another few decades to learn and grow closer to the Lord when our lives might be less busy.

We should desire to be transformed into the image of Christ. If we have no clue who Jesus is because we've never read the gospels or maybe we've never heard the Good News other than an entertaining sermon illustration on Easter a few years ago, then how can we be transformed into His image? (2 Cor. 3:18) How can we acknowledge our need for a Savior unless we actually realized the depths of our sinfulness and how it has separated us from God?

Girl, you need to read your Bible! Not because I'm telling you, but because the Lord has given you a tangible way to know Him, to know about His love for you, to realize your need for a Savior, to know Who your Savior is, and to know who He created you to be. After knowing this, how can you leave your Bible on the shelf any longer and not desire to know truth?

We must also recognize that after all we have learned through the reading and studying of God's Word, we simply cannot keep it to ourselves. What's next? Don't realize all of these things, hold onto them, and refuse to share them with the world as we have been commissioned.

The final words of a dying friend or family member are often profound words of great importance. The last words we have record of that Jesus said before He ascended into heaven were, "you will be my witnesses in Jerusalem, in all Judea and Samaria, and to the ends of the earth." (Acts 1:7-8) It wasn't "Hey! It's been fun, guys. Hope your lives are all better now," while he disappeared into the clouds. He said, *"Go! Share this!"* Do not keep this good news to yourself. Change the world around you.

It starts with you. It starts with you choosing to follow Jesus; it starts with you spending time with and growing closer to the Lord; and then it extends, not because you chose the profession of a pastor or a missionary, but because of who you are as one who has been saved by grace and received the incredible gift of the blood of Jesus washing away your sin. You have been commissioned to do so.

Will it be easy? I won't lie to you and say that it will be. You will not find a long list of Scripture references to support it being as such either. In fact, you'll find quite a bit to the contrary. God has, however, promised to be with you. Just as He was with the Israelites in the wilderness (Ex. 13:21; 15:25; 16:12-15; 17:8-13), just as He was with Shadrach, Meshach, and Abednego in the fiery furnace (Dan. 3:24-29), just as He was with Paul (Acts 16:25-34; 27:21-44), He will be with you.

This is not an easy path. The gate that leads to life is narrow. (Matt. 7:13-14) Be obedient, and do what the Lord has called you to do. Speak truth. Always be ready with an answer for the reason for the hope that is in you. (I Pet. 3:15) Go as you have been commissioned; but also remember that God is the One that changes the hearts of men.

As you progress through the days ahead, do not neglect to be mindful that you are to be the light of the world. (Matt. 5:14-16) As Christ followers, we are intended to stand out. A light doesn't hide; a light makes a difference in the darkness. A light *changes* the environment around it – that cannot be done by hiding the light, but by allowing it to be seen.

"You are the light of the world. A city set on a hill cannot be hidden. Nor do people light a lamp and put it under a basket, but on a stand, and it gives light to all in the house. In the same way, let your light shine before others, so that they may see your good works and give glory to your Father who is in heaven."
Matthew 5:14-16

Practically speaking, how else do we move forward in this challenge to know God's Word? I believe a piece of this simply involves being *intentional* to spend time in the Word. What does that look like? For some of you, it may mean actually scheduling it on your calendar as you create a new habit. For others, it may mean finding a Bible reading plan to keep you on track or even asking a friend to help keep you accountable. Whatever it is you choose to do, may it be purposeful and not an afterthought. May you be richly blessed and find great peace and joy as you spend time in God's Word and grow in your relationship with your Creator and Savior.

WHAT DOES THE BIBLE SAY ABOUT...?

❖ MARRIAGE

Gen. 2:18	Mark 10:5-12	I Cor. 13:4-8
Gen. 2:24	Luke 16:18	Eph. 5:22-33
Mal. 2:16	I Cor. 7:2-13	Col. 3:14
Matt. 5:32	I Cor. 7:15	Col. 3:18-19
Matt. 19:3-9	I Cor. 7:39	I Pet. 3:1-7

❖ WHEN LIFE BEGINS

Job 31:15	Ps. 139:13-16	Jer. 1:5
Ps. 22:10		

❖ FEAR

Josh. 1:9	Ps. 56:3	2 Tim. 1:7
Ps. 23:4	Is. 41:10	I John 4:18
Ps. 27:1	Is. 41:13	
Ps. 34:4	Matt. 10:29-31	

❖ WORRY

Ps. 94:19	Matt. 6:34	John 14:27
Prov. 12:25	Matt. 13:22	Phil. 4:6-7
Matt. 6:25	Luke 12:22-24	I Pet. 5:7

❖ RACE

Acts 10:34-36	Gal. 3:28	I John 2:11
Acts 17:26	Phil. 2:3-4	
Rom.10:12-13	Col. 3:13	

❖ CREATION

Gen. 1:1	Gen. 1:31	John 1:3
Gen. 1:3	Ex.20:11	Col. 1:16
Gen. 1:21	Ps. 33:6	Rev. 4:11
Gen. 1:25-27	Mark 10:6	

❖ PARENTING

Deut. 6:7	Prov. 22:6	Heb. 12:7-11
Ps. 127:3-5	Eph. 6:4	3 John 1:4
Prov. 13:24	Col. 3:21	

❖ FORGIVENESS

Ps. 32:5	Luke 7:44-50	Eph. 1:7
Ps. 103:12	Luke 17:3-4	Eph. 4:31-32
Prov. 28:13	Luke 23:34	Col. 1:13-14
Matt. 5:23-24	Acts 2:38	Col. 3:13
Matt. 6:14-15	Acts 10:43	I John 1:9-10
Matt. 18:21-22	Romans 8:1	I John 2:1
Mark 11:25		

❖ SIN

Prov. 28:13	Rom. 3:23	Col. 3:5-6
Mark 7:20-23	Rom. 6:23	James 4:17-21
John 3:19-21	I Cor. 10:13	James 5:16
Acts 3:19	Gal. 5:19-21	I John 1:7-10
Acts 10:43		

❖ ETERNITY

Deut. 6:7	Prov. 13:24	Eph. 6:4
Ps. 127:3-5	Prov. 22:6	Col. 3:21

NOTES

CHAPTER 3: ME TIME

1. James Gilchrist Lawson, *Cyclopedia of Religious Anecdotes* (Fleming H. Revell Company, 1923), 303.

CHAPTER 4: GOD WANTS ME TO BE HAPPY

1. Corrie Ten Boom, *The Hiding Place* (Grand Rapids, MI: Chosen Books, 2006), 209-210.

CHAPTER 8: THE ROOT OF ALL EVIL

1. Dan Moskowitz, "The 10 Richest People in the World," Investopedia, Oct. 27, 2021, https://www.investopedia.com/articles/investing/012715/5-richest-people-world.asp.
2. "The Richest People of All Time," Love Money, Jun. 28, 2021, https://www.lovemoney.com/gallerylist/51988/the-richest-people-of-all-time.

CHAPTER 11: HOSPITAL FOR SINNERS

1. Ronald F. Youngblood, Nelson's Illustrated Bible Dictionary (Nashville, Tennessee: Thomas Nelson, 1986), 247.

Honey Woods is a child of God, a devoted wife, and a mom to six beautiful children. While she grew up in the church, she didn't fully grasp the depth of her heavenly Father's love until later in life. She has now come to treasure the truth found in the Word of God and desires to share that and the hope of Jesus Christ with the world around her. You can connect with her and learn more at realtruthandhope.com.

Made in United States
Orlando, FL
10 April 2023

31960802R00059